FOR MY BIGGEST
BEAVER FANS—BLAKE,
LIZ, TREVOR, AND CHARLIE.
AND, OF COURSE, HANNA.
(GO, DUCKS!) —K.T.

TO FRANCISCO,
WITH ALL MY LOVE
AND GRATITUDE —L.U.

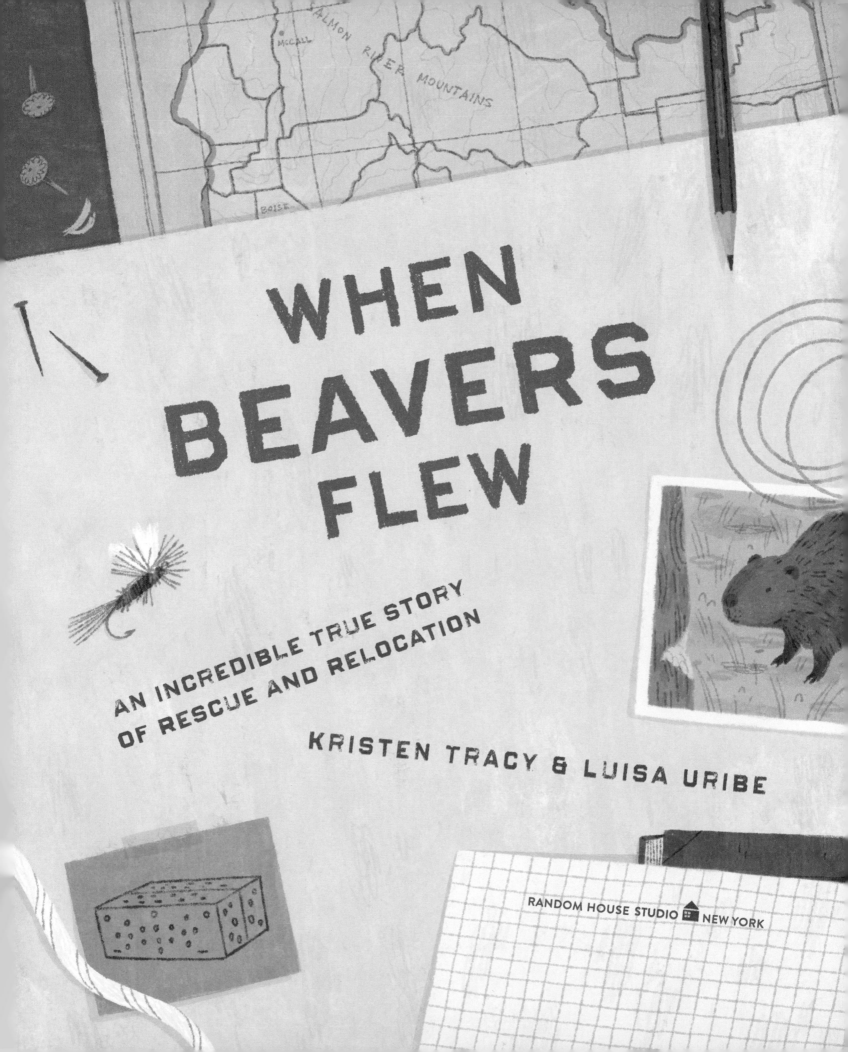

WHEN BEAVERS FLEW

AN INCREDIBLE TRUE STORY OF RESCUE AND RELOCATION

KRISTEN TRACY & LUISA URIBE

RANDOM HOUSE STUDIO ■ NEW YORK

This is a beaver.

This is McCall, Idaho. In 1948, things were booming.

As the mountain town grew, people
found a beaver here and a beaver there.

In fact, they found beavers everywhere.

It was a **BIG, BIG** problem.

An Idaho Fish and Game warden named Elmo Heter knew how to trap beavers, and he came up with a solution.

TRUCK
HORSES
MULES

He'd keep a few beavers in McCall but move the rest to the Chamberlain Basin, where they could build their dams and grow their colonies in a place far away from people.

E. Heter

Elmo knew that without beavers, wetlands and the animals that lived in them would disappear. He hoped to find a balance.

The big mountains surrounding McCall
didn't have roads, which made moving the
semi-aquatic rodents very, very hard.

First, Elmo tried using mules and packhorses.

But the sunlight was too bright, and the beavers had to be constantly watered and cooled. The mules and horses didn't enjoy the journey *or* the passengers. They all turned back.

Elmo needed a new plan.

One day, Elmo considered a different problem. They had too many parachutes left over from World War II. He looked at the surplus parachutes. He thought about the beavers.

He had a wild idea.

FLYING TIME 12.00
COST OF TWO BOXES 2.00

They could parachute-drop the beavers into Idaho's backcountry, returning them to an area the beavers hadn't inhabited in decades. It sounded outrageous, but what if it worked?

Elmo built a special box, full of air holes, designed to pop open when it hit the ground.

Elmo tested it with weights . . .

until he was sure it was safe.

Next, he captured a test beaver and named him Geronimo. He put Geronimo in the box.

And dropped him from a plane.

Over and over.

It worked

and it worked

and it worked.

Using great care, Elmo captured seventy-five more beavers and tagged their ears. He chose to relocate the most troublesome builders, leaving others behind in McCall.

No. 13 – 102 lb
No. 14 – 105 lb
――――
/
max.

He sorted the furry animals
by size and weight.

Then he loaded each pair
into the drop boxes.

And on a day with no
wind, Elmo stacked them
inside the plane.

Into the air and down they flew . . .

. . . aimed toward distant meadows,
mountain lakes, and streams.

Each time a box hit the ground, it sprang open. Box after box. **BONK!**

BONK!

BONK!

A beaver is built to find water.
Elmo hoped they'd all live well and be happy.
Make new places for ducks, swans, and herons to
live. Give moose more bushes and aquatic plants
to eat. Attract muskrats, minks, and otters.

Back at home, Elmo's mind turned often
to those beavers. He thought beaver ponds,
with their cooler and well-oxygenated water,
could increase the number and variety of
frogs, toads, and salamanders in the region.
Plus, Elmo thought beaver dams would be
helpful for salmon and steelhead trout,
by slowing down the rivers and creating
protective pools at the ideal temperature
for their young.

All year, time ticked and Elmo wondered about
those seventy-six beavers loose in the wild world.
He decided it was time to visit. He flew over where
the beavers were dropped. Guess what he saw?

He found the hardworking beavers doing exactly what he'd hoped.

Building dams, capturing water, and making pond and wetland habitat.

Elmo's idea was a total success.

What Geronimo and his seventy-five friends created is part of the largest protected roadless forest in the continental United States.

Today, this is the Chamberlain Basin, now part of the Frank Church–River of No Return Wilderness. And it's populated with beavers once again. Just look at what those beavers built.

AUTHOR'S NOTE

Beavers are important partners for us in fighting climate change by restoring and protecting streams and watersheds. Their hard work improves water quality, reduces flood risk, increases biodiversity, preserves water through droughts, and creates wetland habitat for other animals.

While parachuting some pesky dam-building beavers from one location to another might sound like an extreme idea, it was probably the only one that would have worked. The townspeople in McCall saw the beavers as a nuisance and most likely didn't appreciate their ecological value. The beavers were destroying new construction and damaging orchards and farmland. The people had pushed into beaver habitat, and the beavers weren't going to suddenly change their behavior or abandon their colonies. You needed somebody like Elmo, who had both the ingenuity and the will to save these beavers *and* put them in a location where beavers needed to be. The Chamberlain Basin needed beavers to return to the region and help balance its ecosystem, after they had been hunted to near extinction in the early 1800s. Elmo understood these beavers' environmental importance, so he went to great lengths to save them.

People move animals for a variety of reasons. The animals may be deemed a nuisance, or the animal population elsewhere may need to be reestablished or grow. The word for moving animals from one habitat to another is *translocation.* Despite the good intentions, recent studies have shown that in many cases, moving these animals can cause more harm than good. Translocated animals often have to compete with other species for food and other resources in unfamiliar surroundings.

Idaho's beaver story has a happy ending because Elmo selected an ideal habitat where beavers could thrive, and it also lacked predators. (Like beavers, predators had also been hunted to near extinction in this region.) Equally important, Elmo moved so many animals that they were able to maintain their social relationships. Although one unfortunate beaver managed to climb out of its box midfall, all the others miraculously survived.

The Chamberlain Basin is now part of the Frank Church–River of No Return Wilderness Area—the largest unbroken wilderness in the lower forty-eight states, encompassing 2,366,757 acres. It's named after Idaho's Senator Frank Church, who played a key role in passing legislation to protect important wilderness areas and the animals that live there.

Today, this area is protected. You need a permit to visit many parts of it, including the Middle Fork of the Salmon River, where you can find wildlife such as black bears, moose, mule deer, steelhead trout, and western toads. This rugged mountain landscape was once the home of the Tukudika (the Sheep Eaters), an indigenous people who inhabited the land for nine thousand years.

If you look carefully at the page where Elmo is trying to use mules and packhorses to move the beavers, you will see that Luisa Uribe has depicted a piece of Tukudika artwork on the boulder behind the mule on the far right.

We know a lot more now about the ecological benefits of beavers and their dams than people did in 1948, when this story took place. More and more, we're able to use coexistence techniques to peacefully solve conflicts with beavers. For example, tree trunks can be coated with sand to discourage chewing, and pipes can be inserted into dams to control water levels.

SELECTED SOURCES

Crew, Bec. "Why 76 Beavers Were Forced to Skydive into the Idaho Wilderness in 1948." *Scientific American,* January 29, 2015.

Goldfarb, Ben. *Eager: The Surprising, Secret Life of Beavers and Why They Matter.* White River Junction, VT: Chelsea Green Publishing, 2018.

Heter, Elmo W. "Transplanting Beavers by Airplane and Parachute." *The Journal of Wildlife Management,* April 1950.

Hood, Glynnis. *The Beaver Manifesto.* Victoria, BC, Canada: Rocky Mountain Books, 2011.

Idaho Fish and Game. *Fur for the Future* (film). youtube.com /watch?v=APLz2bTprMA

Koenigsberg, Sarah, dir. *The Beaver Believers* (film). Tensegrity Productions, 2018.

Mistretta, Anne Marie. "The Mountain Shoshone: A History of the Sheep Eater Indians in the Big Sky Area." *Mountain Outlaw* magazine, summer 2012. www.mtoutlaw.com/summer-2012

National Park Service. "The Tukudika Indians." nps.gov /yell/learn/historyculture/the-tukudika-indians.htm

Sherriff, Lucy. "Why Beavers Were Parachuted into the Idaho Wilderness 73 Years Ago." *National Geographic,* September 2021.

Wagner, Laura. "WATCH: Long-Lost Parachuting Beaver Footage from 1950." NPR, *The Two-Way,* October 22, 2015. npr.org /sections/thetwo-way/2015/10/22/450958213/watch-long-lost -parachuting-beaver-footage-from-1950

Wright, Samantha. "Parachuting Beavers into Idaho's Wilderness? Yes, It Really Happened." Boise State Public Radio News, January 14, 2015.

Zorthian, Julia. "The True History Behind Idaho's Parachuting Beavers." Time.com, October 23, 2015. time.com/4084997/parachuting-beavers-history

ELMO HETER, PICTURED WEARING SUNGLASSES, AND HIS COMPANION PLACE A BEAVER IN A WOODEN CRATE TO PREPARE FOR A PARACHUTE DROP.

ACKNOWLEDGMENTS

Many thanks again to my always-awesome agent for nearly twenty years, Sara Crowe. I'm also grateful to my brilliant editor, Lee Wade, who helped me shape this book into its best self; to Estefania Valencia, who guided it through its final stages; to Jenny Golub, who masterfully copyedited the manuscript; and to Rachael Cole for her detailed art direction. Big thanks to everybody at the Idaho Department of Fish and Game who answered all my beaver questions, including Christy Hooper, Cory Mosby, and Sharon Clark. (Sharon also helped locate and digitize *Fur for the Future,* the long-lost film about the parachuting beavers, which reached the internet in 2015.) I'm also deeply grateful to Ben Goldfarb for taking the time to thoughtfully answer my questions. Of course, I only made half of this book. Huge thanks to Luisa Uribe, who brought the story to life with illustrations that are so accurate and stunning that I want to turn them into a pantsuit and wear this book to special events and also, when the time comes, be buried in it. On that note, thank you to my family, who make my life worth living—especially my husband, Brian Evenson, and our son, Max (a true beaver fan). And special thanks to my father-in-law, Bill Evenson, who helped answer my fish and stream questions. And extra-special thanks to my parents, Carl and Patti, who took me camping as a child and introduced me to the Idaho wilderness. Those memories stay with me always.